JumpStart Your Transportation Business

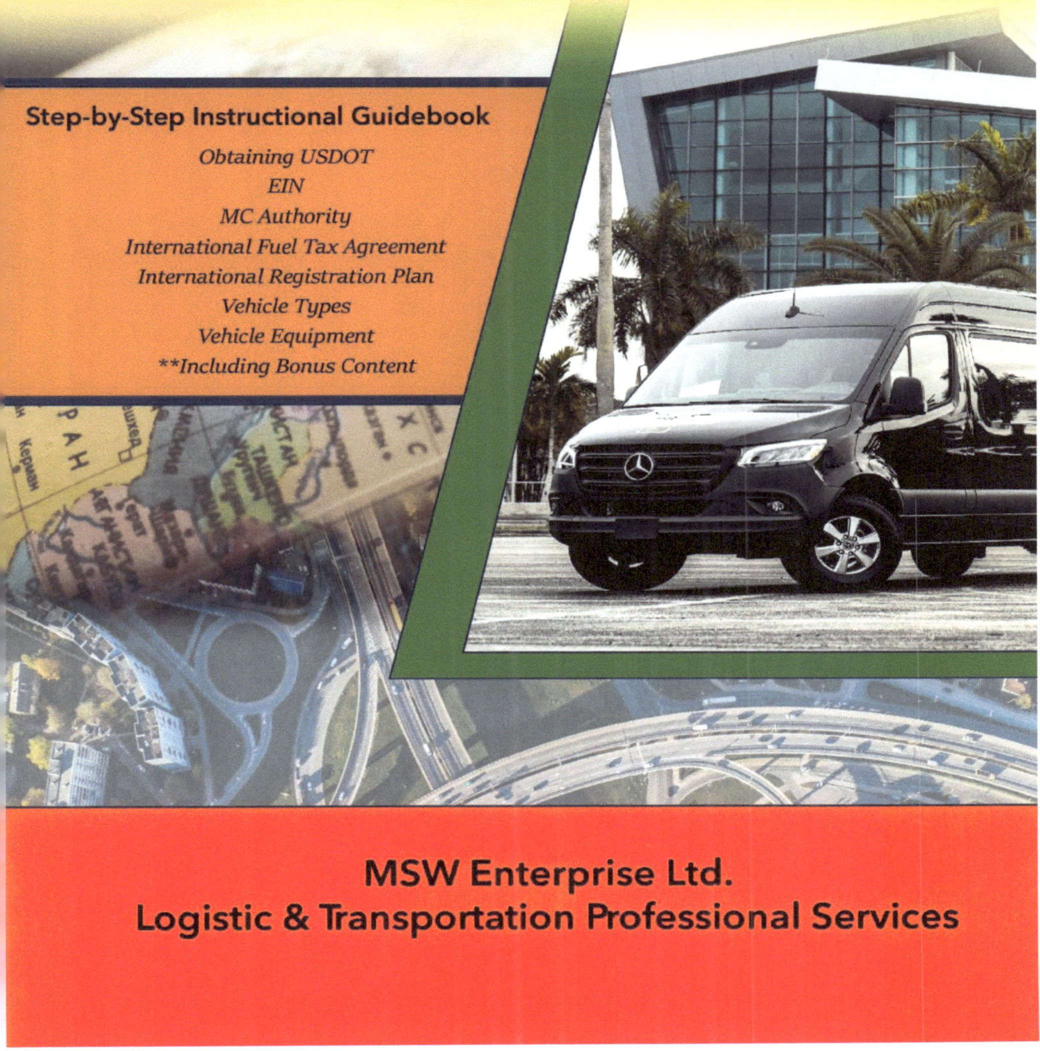

Step-by-Step Instructional Guidebook

Obtaining USDOT
EIN
MC Authority
International Fuel Tax Agreement
International Registration Plan
Vehicle Types
Vehicle Equipment
**Including Bonus Content

MSW Enterprise Ltd.
Logistic & Transportation Professional Services

So, your ready to enter the world of entrepreneurship! Setting up a business structure is a critical decision for any entrepreneur or business owner because it impacts nearly every aspect of the business, from legal liability to taxes, management, and operational flexibility. The business structure determines the extent to which your personal assets are protected from business liabilities. For example, forming a Limited Liability Company (LLC) or a Corporation provides limited liability protection, meaning your personal assets (like your home or savings) are generally protected if your business faces lawsuits or debts. In contrast, in a sole proprietorship or partnership, the owners have unlimited liability, meaning personal assets can be used to satisfy business debts.

Different business structures are taxed differently. For instance, a sole proprietorship and partnership have pass-through taxation, where business income is reported on the owner's personal tax return, and the business itself is not taxed separately. In contrast, a corporation (especially a C-corporation) is taxed as a separate legal entity, which can lead to double taxation (once at the corporate level and again on dividends paid to shareholders). Some structures, like an S-Corporation or an LLC, offer tax flexibility, allowing owners to choose how they want the business to be taxed (e.g., as a pass-through entity or as a corporation).

The structure determines how the business is managed and who has control. In a sole proprietorship, the owner has full control over all decisions. In a partnership, decision-making is shared among partners, which requires clear agreements on roles and responsibilities. While Corporations and LLC structures have formal management structures, with corporations typically having a board of directors and officers, and LLCs having managers or managing members. This can help in clearly defining roles and responsibilities.

Each structure has different legal and regulatory requirements. For instance, corporations must adhere to more stringent regulations, including filing annual reports and holding shareholder meetings. LLCs have fewer requirements but still need to comply with state laws. More formal structures like corporations require detailed record-keeping and documentation to maintain compliance, which can be burdensome but is essential for legal protection and transparency.

A well-structured business may be seen as more credible and trustworthy, which can be beneficial in establishing relationships with customers, suppliers, and lenders.

Choosing the right business structure is foundational to the success and longevity of your business. It influences your legal obligations, tax liabilities, operational flexibility, and the ability to raise capital. Making an informed decision about your business structure requires careful consideration of your business goals, the level of risk you're willing to assume, and the regulatory environment in which you operate. Consulting with legal and financial professionals can help ensure that you choose the structure that best aligns with your business needs and future plans.

Registering Your Business with Your Secretary of State

Registering a business with the Secretary of State (SoS) may vary slightly depending on the state or country where you are registering. Registering your business with the Secretary of State (SoS) is a crucial step in establishing and legally operating your business.

Here are the main reasons why it is necessary to register your business:

- Registering your business with the Secretary of State formally establishes its existence as a legal entity. This is especially important for business structures like corporations and LLCs, which are separate legal entities from their owners. Registration provides legal recognition and protects the personal assets of the owners from business liabilities.
- Each state has specific laws and regulations governing the formation and operation of businesses. Registering with the SoS ensures that your business complies with these laws, including requirements for business names, governance structures, and filings.
- Registering your business name with the Secretary of State can provide some level of protection in your jurisdiction. It prevents other businesses from registering under the same or similar names, which helps establish your brand identity and prevents confusion among consumers.
- Registration often involves obtaining a state tax identification number or employer identification number (EIN) from the IRS. These numbers are necessary for paying state taxes, sales taxes (if applicable), and for employment tax purposes.
- Many banks, vendors, and potential business partners may require proof of your business's legal status (such as Articles of Incorporation or Articles of Organization) before entering into contracts or agreements with your company.
- Registered businesses may have easier access to certain government programs, grants, loans, and services that are available to businesses within the state.
- Regularly filing required documents (such as annual reports or statements) with the Secretary of State helps your business maintain good standing. Good standing is often a requirement for renewing licenses, maintaining business contracts, and conducting business transactions.
- Registering your business ensures that you are operating within the legal framework of your state. It provides clarity on legal responsibilities, helps protect your business interests, and ensures compliance with state regulations.

Overall, registering your business with the Secretary of State is essential for establishing its legal presence, complying with state laws, protecting your business name, accessing services, and maintaining good standing in your jurisdiction. It is a fundamental step in laying the groundwork for a successful and legally compliant business operation.

Registering Your Business with Your Secretary of State

1. Choose a Business Structure: Before registering, decide on the legal structure of your business:
   - Sole Proprietorship: Owned and operated by one person.
   - Partnership: Owned by two or more people who share responsibilities and profits.
   - Limited Liability Company (LLC): Provides limited liability to owners (members) and flexibility in management.
   - Corporation: A separate legal entity from its owners (shareholders) with limited liability protection.

2. Choose a Business Name: Select a unique name for your business that complies with naming rules and is available in your jurisdiction. You may need to check the availability of the name through the SoS website or office.

3. Register with the Secretary of State
   - Gather Required Information: Prepare information such as business name, business structure, address, names and addresses of owners/officers, and purpose of the business.
   - File Formation Documents: Complete and file the appropriate formation documents with the Secretary of State's office. This may include Articles of Incorporation for corporations, Articles of Organization for LLCs, or other forms depending on your business structure.
   - Pay Filing Fees: There are usually fees associated with filing your formation documents. Check the SoS website for fee information and payment methods.
   - Publication Requirements: In some states, you may be required to publish a notice of your intent to form a business entity in a local newspaper. Make sure to comply with any publication requirements if applicable.
   - Once your documents are filed and fees are paid, wait for approval from the Secretary of State. This process can take several weeks, depending on your jurisdiction.

4. Obtain Necessary Permits and Licenses: After your business is registered with the Secretary of State, you may need to obtain additional permits or licenses to legally operate your business. This may include local business licenses, industry-specific permits, sales tax permits, i.e. Completed FMCSA registration requirements.

5. Maintain Compliance
   - Annual Reports: Many states require businesses to file annual reports or statements and pay renewal fees to maintain active status.
   - Ongoing Compliance: Stay compliant with tax obligations, regulatory requirements, and any changes to business information (e.g., changes in ownership or address).

Additional Tips:

- ❖ Use Resources: Consult the Secretary of State's website or contact their office directly for specific instructions and forms relevant to your jurisdiction.
- ❖ Consider Legal Advice: Depending on the complexity of your business structure or operations, you may want to consult with a business attorney or tax advisor to ensure compliance and understand legal implications.

Registering Your Business with Your Secretary of State

- ☐ Choose a Business Structure

- ☐ Choose a Business Name

- ☐ Register with the Secretary of State

- ☐ Obtain Necessary Permits and Licenses

- ☐ Maintain Compliance

 **Please be sure to follow the details as outlined in your Start Your Transportation Guidebook**

Obtaining Your Business EIN for Free

Obtaining an Employer Identification Number (EIN) from the IRS (Internal Revenue Service) is a necessary step for many businesses and organizations, particularly those that plan to hire employees or have certain tax obligations. An EIN is a unique nine-digit number assigned by the IRS (Internal Revenue Service) to businesses and other entities for tax purposes.

Why Your Business Needs An EIN Number

- An EIN is necessary for filing various business tax returns with the IRS. This includes income tax returns (for corporations, partnerships, and certain LLCs), employment tax returns (such as Form 941 for payroll taxes), excise tax returns, and certain information returns.
- If your business plans to hire employees, you need an EIN to withhold federal income taxes, Social Security taxes, and Medicare taxes from employee wages. It's also used for reporting employment taxes to the IRS.
- Most banks require an EIN to open a business bank account. It helps identify your business for financial transactions and ensures compliance with banking regulations.
- Many states and local jurisdictions require an EIN when applying for business licenses, permits, or registrations. It helps verify your business's identity and tax status.
- Suppliers, vendors, and other business partners may request your EIN for tax reporting purposes, especially if they provide goods or services to your business.
- An EIN is used for official correspondence with the IRS regarding your business taxes, filings, and compliance issues.
- For legal entities such as corporations, LLCs, and partnerships, an EIN helps establish the business as a separate legal entity from its owners. This provides limited liability protection and distinguishes personal and business finances.
- If your business establishes retirement plans (such as a 401(k)) or certain types of trusts, an EIN is required for IRS reporting and compliance.

An EIN is essential for businesses and entities to fulfill tax obligations, hire employees, open bank accounts, obtain licenses, and conduct various business transactions. It serves as a unique identifier for your business with federal and state authorities, ensuring compliance with tax laws and regulations.

Obtaining Your Business EIN for Free

Quick Easy Steps to getting your business EIN:

- ✓ Determine Eligibility: Before applying for an EIN, ensure your business or entity is eligible. Most types of businesses, including sole proprietorships, partnerships, corporations, LLCs, estates, trusts, and certain nonprofits, qualify for an EIN.

- ✓ Prepare Information
  - Gather the following information about your business or entity:
    - Legal name of the entity (as it appears on official documents)
    - Trade name or "Doing Business As" (DBA) name, if applicable
    - Business address
    - Type of entity (e.g., sole proprietorship, corporation, LLC)
    - Reason for applying (e.g., starting a new business, hiring employees, banking purposes)

- ✓ Choose Your Application Method: there are several ways to apply for an EIN:
  Online Application:
  - Go to the IRS website and use the online EIN Assistant.
  - Complete the application by answering questions about your business or entity.
  - Submit the application electronically. Once validated, you will receive your EIN immediately.

  Apply by Fax:
  - Download Form SS-4, Application for Employer Identification Number, from the IRS website.
  - Complete the form with required information.
  - Fax the completed Form SS-4 to the appropriate IRS fax number (based on your state).

  Apply by Mail:
  - Download Form SS-4 from the IRS website.
  - Complete the form with required information.
  - Mail the completed Form SS-4 to the appropriate IRS address (based on your state).

- ✓ Submit the Application
  - For online applications, submit electronically through the IRS website.
  - For fax or mail applications, ensure all required information is accurate and complete before submission.

- ✓ Receive Your EIN
  - If applying online, you will receive your EIN immediately upon successful submission and validation of your application.
  - If applying by fax or mail, it may take up to several weeks to receive your EIN. Once processed, the IRS will mail your EIN confirmation letter to the address provided on your application.

- ✓ Keep Your EIN Secure
  - Store your EIN confirmation letter in a safe place. You will need it for tax filing purposes, opening bank accounts, applying for licenses and permits, and other business transactions.

Obtaining your FREE EIN

Quick Easy Steps to getting your business EIN:

- ✓ Determine Eligibility: Before applying for an EIN, ensure your business or entity is eligible. Most types of businesses, including sole proprietorships, partnerships, corporations, LLCs, estates, trusts, and certain nonprofits, qualify for an EIN.

- ✓ Prepare Information
  - ❏ Gather the following information about your business or entity:
    - ○ Legal name of the entity (as it appears on official documents)
    - ○ Trade name or "Doing Business As" (DBA) name, if applicable
    - ○ Business address
    - ○ Type of entity (e.g., sole proprietorship, corporation, LLC)
    - ○ Reason for applying (e.g., starting a new business, hiring employees, banking purposes)

- ✓ Choose Your Application Method: there are several ways to apply for an EIN:
  Online Application:
  - ➤ Go to the IRS website and use the online EIN Assistant.
  - ➤ Complete the application by answering questions about your business or entity.
  - ➤ Submit the application electronically. Once validated, you will receive your EIN immediately.

  Apply by Fax:
  - ➤ Download Form SS-4, Application for Employer Identification Number, from the IRS website.
  - ➤ Complete the form with required information.
  - ➤ Fax the completed Form SS-4 to the appropriate IRS fax number (based on your state).

  Apply by Mail:
  - ➤ Download Form SS-4 from the IRS website.
  - ➤ Complete the form with required information.
  - ➤ Mail the completed Form SS-4 to the appropriate IRS address (based on your state).

- ✓ Submit the Application
  - ❏ For online applications, submit electronically through the IRS website.
  - ❏ For fax or mail applications, ensure all required information is accurate and complete before submission.

- ✓ Receive Your EIN
  - ❏ If applying online, you will receive your EIN immediately upon successful submission and validation of your application.
  - ❏ If applying by fax or mail, it may take up to several weeks to receive your EIN. Once processed, the IRS will mail your EIN confirmation letter to the address provided on your application.

- ✓ Keep Your EIN Secure
  - ❏ Store your EIN confirmation letter in a safe place. You will need it for tax filing purposes, opening bank accounts, applying for licenses and permits, and other business transactions.

Dun & Bradstreet (D&B) Number

A Dun & Bradstreet (D&B) number, specifically a D-U-N-S® Number, is a unique nine-digit identifier used to establish a business credit file with Dun & Bradstreet. While it's not typically required by government agencies such as the FMCSA (Federal Motor Carrier Safety Administration) for basic registrations like obtaining a USDOT number or MC authority, it may be requested or recommended for several reasons. Obtaining a D-U-N-S® Number from Dun & Bradstreet typically does not cost anything for most businesses, and in fact, the vast majority of businesses, obtaining a basic D-U-N-S® Number is free of charge. It's important to keep in mind, Dun & Bradstreet offers additional services and products that businesses may choose to purchase. These could include credit monitoring services, business credit reports, marketing lists, and more advanced business insights. These services are optional and come with associated costs. Finally, it's important to note that while the D-U-N-S® Number is free to obtain initially, businesses are responsible for keeping their information updated with Dun & Bradstreet and there may be costs associated with certain verification or enhancement services offered by Dun & Bradstreet.

Reasons Your Business May Need A D&B Number

- ❖ D&B is a prominent business credit bureau that collects and maintains information on businesses worldwide. Having a D-U-N-S® Number allows D&B to create a credit profile for your business, which can be accessed by lenders, suppliers, and potential partners to evaluate your creditworthiness and business stability.

- ❖ Government agencies, large corporations, and other entities may require a D-U-N-S® Number as part of their vendor registration process. It helps them assess the financial health and reliability of the businesses they work with.

- ❖ The D-U-N-S® Number is recognized globally as a standard business identifier. If your business engages in international transactions or partnerships, having a D-U-N-S® Number can facilitate these interactions by providing a standardized way to identify your business.

- ❖ Some organizations use D&B's database to verify business information such as address, ownership, and operational status. Having a D-U-N-S® Number ensures that your business details are accurately represented in these databases.

- ❖ Some business opportunities, including government contracts or grants, may require a D-U-N-S® Number as part of the eligibility criteria. It can also open doors to networking opportunities and business development initiatives.

While a D-U-N-S® Number is not universally required for all business registrations, it serves as a valuable tool for establishing your business's credit profile, enhancing credibility in business transactions, and accessing certain business opportunities and resources. It's especially useful for businesses looking to build and maintain relationships with larger corporations and government entities.

Dun & Bradstreet (D&B) Number
How to Quick Guide on Obtaining Your D&B Number

1. Visit the Dun & Bradstreet website: Go to the official D&B website (dnb.com).

2. Navigate to the D-U-N-S® Number page: Look for the section specifically about obtaining a D-U-N-S® Number. This is typically found under the "Business Credit Solutions" or "Get a D-U-N-S® Number" tab.

3. Check if you already have a D-U-N-S® Number: Some businesses may already have a D-U-N-S® Number assigned to them if they have been previously registered or if they are publicly listed. You can check for an existing D-U-N-S® Number using the search function on the D&B website.

4. Register for a new D-U-N-S® Number: If your business does not have a D-U-N-S® Number, you will need to register for one. This usually involves filling out an online form with information about your business, such as legal name, address, ownership structure, and contact details.

5. Verification and review: Dun & Bradstreet will verify the information provided and may contact you for additional details or documentation to confirm your business's identity and legitimacy.

6. Receive your D-U-N-S® Number: Once the verification process is complete and your application is approved, Dun & Bradstreet will assign a unique D-U-N-S® Number to your business. This number is free of charge for most businesses.

7. Use your D-U-N-S® Number: After receiving your D-U-N-S® Number, you can start using it for various purposes, such as applying for business credit, establishing credibility with suppliers and partners, and registering with government agencies.

8. Keep your information updated: It's important to keep your business information current with Dun & Bradstreet to ensure the accuracy of your D-U-N-S® Number profile.

By following these steps, you can obtain a Dun & Bradstreet number and leverage it to enhance your business's reputation and financial standing.

DUN & BRADSTREET PLANNER

START DATE: **DUE DATE:**

1. Visit the Dun & Bradstreet website: Go to the official D&B website (dnb.com).

2. Navigate to the D-U-N-S® Number page: Look for the section specifically about obtaining a D-U-N-S® Number. This is typically found under the "Business Credit Solutions" or "Get a D-U-N-S® Number" tab.

3. Check if you already have a D-U-N-S® Number: Some businesses may already have a D-U-N-S® Number assigned to them if they have been previously registered or if they are publicly listed. You can check for an existing D-U-N-S® Number using the search function on the D&B website.

4. Register for a new D-U-N-S® Number: If your business does not have a D-U-N-S® Number, you will need to register for one. This usually involves filling out an online form with information about your business, such as legal name, address, ownership structure, and contact details.

5. Verification and review: Dun & Bradstreet will verify the information provided and may contact you for additional details or documentation to confirm your business's identity and legitimacy.

6. Receive your D-U-N-S® Number: Once the verification process is complete and your application is approved, Dun & Bradstreet will assign a unique D-U-N-S® Number to your business. This number is free of charge for most businesses.

7. Use your D-U-N-S® Number: After receiving your D-U-N-S® Number, you can start using it for various purposes, such as applying for business credit, establishing credibility with suppliers and partners, and registering with government agencies.

8. Keep your information updated: It's important to keep your business information current with Dun & Bradstreet to ensure the accuracy of your D-U-N-S® Number profile.

Using the Unified Carrier Registration (UCR)

The purpose of the Unified Carrier Registration (UCR) program is to ensure compliance and financial support for motor carriers, motor private carriers, brokers, freight forwarders, and leasing companies operating in interstate commerce within the United States and Canada. The UCR program was established as a process for carriers and other entities operating in multiple states. Qualifying entities must register annually with the UCR program. This includes providing basic information about their business operations and paying a registration fee based on the size of their fleet. Compliance with the UCR program is mandatory for motor carriers, brokers, and others engaged in interstate commerce. It ensures that these entities contribute financially to the regulation and oversight of their operations across state lines. *Remember if you're an intrastate motor carrier this is not applicable.* *

Steps on how to use UCR effectively:

1. **Determine UCR Requirements:** Confirm if your business meets the criteria requiring UCR registration. Generally, interstate motor carriers, freight forwarders, brokers, and leasing companies must register. Some carriers may be exempt based on vehicle types or operations. Check if any exemptions apply to your business.
2. **Register for UCR**
    - Visit the official UCR registration website to begin the registration process.
    - If you are a new user, create an account on the UCR website. If you already have an account, log in using your credentials.
3. **Complete the Registration**
    - Enter required business and vehicle information, including:
        - Business name, address, and contact information.
        - USDOT number (if applicable).
        - Number of commercial motor vehicles (CMVs) in your fleet.
        - Total gross vehicle weight rating (GVWR) of your CMVs.
4. **Calculate Fees**
    - Determine the appropriate fee based on the size of your fleet:
    - Fees are based on the number of qualifying commercial motor vehicles (CMVs) that you operate.
    - Use the fee calculator provided on the UCR website to estimate your registration fees.
5. **Submit Payment**
    - Choose a payment method (credit card, electronic check, etc.) to submit your registration fees.
    - Upon successful payment, you will receive a confirmation of your registration.
6. **Receive Proof of UCR Registration**
7. **Display your UCR registration receipt or certificate in each registered vehicle.**
8. **Renew UCR Registration Annually**

Additional Tips
- *UCR registration is valid for one calendar year (January 1st to December 31st).*
- *Ensure timely renewal before the expiration date to avoid penalties or disruptions in operations.*
- *Maintain Compliance and Records*
- *Keep copies of your UCR registration certificate and receipts for auditing purposes.*
- *Update your registration with any changes to business details, fleet size, or operations as needed.*
- *Regularly check for updates and changes to UCR regulations to maintain compliance.*

By following these steps and staying informed about UCR requirements, you can effectively use UCR interstate registration to operate legally and compliantly as a commercial motor carrier across state lines in the United States.

UNIFIED CARRIER REGISTRATION TO DO LIST

date

Steps on how to use UCR effectively:	
1.	Determine UCR Requirements: Confirm if your business meets the criteria requiring UCR registration. Generally, interstate motor carriers, freight forwarders, brokers, and leasing companies must register. Some carriers may be exempt based on vehicle types or operations. Check if any exemptions apply to your business.
2.	**Register for UCR**
	☐ Visit the official UCR registration website to begin the registration process.
	☐ If you are a new user, create an account on the UCR website. If you already have an account, log in using your credentials.
3.	**Complete the Registration**
	☐ Enter required business and vehicle information, including:
	• Business name, address, and contact information.
	• USDOT number (if applicable).
	• Number of commercial motor vehicles (CMVs) in your fleet.
	• Total gross vehicle weight rating (GVWR) of your CMVs.
4.	**Calculate Fees**
	☐ Determine the appropriate fee based on the size of your fleet:
	☐ Fees are based on the number of qualifying commercial motor vehicles (CMVs) that you operate.
	☐ Use the fee calculator provided on the UCR website to estimate your registration fees.
5.	**Submit Payment**
	☐ Choose a payment method (credit card, electronic check, etc.) to submit your registration fees.
	☐ Upon successful payment, you will receive a confirmation of your registration.
6.	Receive Proof of UCR Registration
7.	Display your UCR registration receipt or certificate in each registered vehicle.
8.	Renew UCR Registration Annually

Obtaining Your USDOT Registration

Registering with the Federal Motor Carrier Safety Administration (FMCSA) to obtain your USDOT number involves several steps. By following these steps, you can successfully register with the FMCSA and obtain your USDOT number, allowing you to legally operate commercial vehicles across state lines in the United States. Here's a guide to help you through the process:

1. Explore if You Need a USDOT Number
    - ☐ Motor Carriers: If you operate a commercial vehicle transporting cargo or passengers across state lines, you generally need a USDOT number.
    - ☐ Commercial Vehicles: This includes vehicles with a gross vehicle weight rating (GVWR) or gross combination weight rating (GCWR) of 10,001 pounds or more, vehicles transporting hazardous materials requiring placarding, and vehicles designed to transport 16 or more passengers (including the driver).

Do I Need a USDOT Number?
Find Out Now

2. Prepare Information
    Ensure you have the following information before starting the registration process:
    - ☐ Business name (if applicable) and address
    - ☐ Contact information (phone number, email)
    - ☐ Type of operation (e.g., motor carrier, broker, freight forwarder)
    - ☐ Principal place of business
    - ☐ Information about any associated companies or subsidiaries

3. Create a FMCSA Portal Account
   Visit the FMCSA's Unified Registration System (URS) online portal and create an account:
   - Go to the FMCSA URS website: [FMCSA URS](https://www.fmcsa.dot.gov/urs)
   - Click on "Register/Update/Reinstate" and follow the prompts to create an account.

4. Complete the Registration
   Once you have an account, log in and complete the online registration form:
   - Enter all required information accurately.
   - Verify and review your information before submitting.

5. Pay Registration Fee (if applicable)
   Depending on your specific situation, there may be a registration fee. Payment options will be provided during the registration process.

6. Receive Your USDOT Number
   After completing the registration process and payment (if required), you will receive your USDOT number immediately. This number serves as a unique identifier for your commercial vehicle operations.

7. Display Your USDOT Number
   Display your USDOT number on all commercial vehicles as required by FMCSA regulations. This typically involves placing it on both sides of the vehicle, along with other required markings if applicable.

Additional Tips:
- *Keep Information Updated***: It's important to keep your registration information up to date, especially if there are changes to your business structure, address, or contact information.
- *Compliance and Safety***: Familiarize yourself with FMCSA regulations regarding safety and compliance to ensure your operations meet federal standards.

OBTAINING YOUR USDOT NUMBER

WEEK at a glance

Mon	Explore if You Need a USDOT Number
Tue	Prepare your information and ensure you have the needed information before starting the registration process
Wed	Create a FMCSA Portal Account
Thurs	Complete the Registration
Fri	Pay Registration Fee (if applicable)
Sat	Receive Your USDOT Number
Sun	Display Your USDOT Number

Obtaining Your Motor Carrier Authority

Obtaining MC (Motor Carrier) authority from the Federal Motor Carrier Safety Admin stration (FMCSA) involves several steps to legally operate as a motor carrier in the United States. Below is the guide to help you through the process:

- ✓ Determine if You Need MC Authority
    - ☐ Motor Carrier: If you intend to transport regulated commodities (property or passengers) as a for-hire carrier across state lines or internationally, you generally r eed MC authority.
    - ☐ Type of Authority: Depending on your specific operations, you may need different types of authority:
    - ☐ MC Number: This is required for interstate for-hire transportation of regulated property (except household goods).
    - ☐ FF Number: If you plan to transport household goods across state lines for compensation, you need an additional Household Goods Motor Carrier (HM) authority (FF Number).

Obtaining Your Motor Carrier Authority

Types of Authority

- **Motor Carrier of Property (except Household Goods):** authorized for-hire Motor Carrier that transports regulated commodities (except household goods) for the general public in exchange for payment.
- **Motor Carrier of Household Goods (HHG - Moving Companies):** authorized for-hire Motor Carrier that transports only household goods for the general public in exchange for payment.
- **Broker of Property (except Household Goods):** receives payment for arranging the transportation of property (excluding household goods) belonging to others by using an authorized Motor Carrier.
- **Broker of Household Goods (HHG):** receives payment for arranging the transportation of household goods belonging to others by using an authorized Motor Carrier.
- **United States-based Enterprise Carrier of International Cargo (except Household Goods):** transports international cargo (excluding household goods) and is headquartered in the United States but is owned or controlled (greater than 55%) by a Mexican citizen or resident alien.
- **United States-based Enterprise Carrier of International Household Goods:** transports international household goods and is headquartered in the United States but is owned or controlled (greater than 55%) by a Mexican citizen or resident alien.
- **Freight Forwarder Authority:** freight forwarders arrange transportation of goods by FMCSA-licensed carriers.
- **Motor Passenger Carrier Authority:** Passenger transportation & vehicle registration.
- **Non-North America-Domiciled Motor Carriers:** carriers based outside of North America (specifically the United States, Canada, and Mexico) who operate commercial motor vehicles within North America.
- **Mexico-based Carriers for Motor Carrier Authority to Operate Beyond U.S. Municipalities and Commercial Zones on the U.S.-Mexico Border:** transport within US, outside Mexico borders.
- **Mexican Certificate of Registration for Foreign Motor Carriers and Foreign Motor Private Carriers:** certificate serves as legal authorization for foreign motor carriers (companies transporting goods for hire) and motor private carriers (individuals or companies transporting their own goods) to operate within Mexican territory.

Obtaining Your Motor Carrier Authority

1. Prepare Information
    Ensure you have the following information before starting the registration process:
    - ☐ Business name (if applicable) and address
    - ☐ Contact information (phone number, email)
    - ☐ Type of operation (e.g., motor carrier, broker, freight forwarder)
    - ☐ Principal place of business
    - ☐ Tax Identification Number (TIN) or Employer Identification Number (EIN)
    - ☐ Information about any associated companies or subsidiaries

2. Create a FMCSA Portal Account
    Visit the FMCSA's Unified Registration System (URS) online portal and create an account:
    - ☐ Go to the FMCSA URS website: [FMCSA URS](https://www.fmcsa.dot.gov/urs)
    - ☐ Click on "Register/Update/Reinstate" and follow the prompts to create an account.

3. After logging in, complete the application for MC authority:
    - ☐ Select the appropriate authority type (MC or FF)
    - ☐ Enter all required information accurately
    - ☐ Provide details about your business operations, including the types of commodities you intend to transport (if applicable).

Types of Commodities

- ➢ Agricultural Commodities:
    - o Grains (wheat, corn, rice, etc.)
    - o Oilseeds (soybeans, rapeseed, etc.)
    - o Livestock (cattle, pigs, poultry, etc.)
    - o Dairy products (milk, cheese, butter, etc.)
    - o Fruits and vegetables
- ➢ Energy Commodities:
    - o Crude oil
    - o Natural gas
    - o Coal
    - o Electricity
- ➢ Metals:
    - o Precious metals (gold, silver, platinum, etc.)
    - o Industrial metals (copper, aluminum, zinc, etc.)
    - o Rare earth metals
- ➢ Soft Commodities:
    - o Coffee
    - o Cocoa
    - o Sugar
    - o Cotton
- ➢ Chemicals and Fertilizers:
    - o Petrochemicals
    - o Fertilizers (urea, phosphates, etc.)
    - o Industrial chemicals (chlorine, ammonia, etc.)
- ➢ Forest Products:
    - o Timber
    - o Paper products
    - o Wood pulp
- ➢ Processed Foods and Beverages:
    - o Packaged foods
    - o Beverages (soft drinks, juices, alcoholic beverages, etc.)
- ➢ Textiles and Apparel:
    - o Cotton yarn
    - o Textile fabrics
    - o Clothing and apparel items
- ➢ Plastics and Polymers
    - o Polyethylene

- Polypropylene
- PVC (polyvinyl chloride)

➤ Construction Materials:
- Cement
- Steel
- Bricks and tiles

➤ Livestock and Animal Products:
- Meat (beef, pork, poultry, etc.)
- Leather
- Wool

➤ Pharmaceuticals and Medical Supplies:
- Prescription drugs
- Medical equipment

➤ Consumer Goods:
- Electronics
- Household appliances
- Automobiles and automotive parts

➤ Waste and Scrap Materials:
- Scrap metal
- Recycled paper
- Plastic scrap

➤ Water:
- Bottled water
- Bulk water transportation

4. Designate Process Agents: a processing agent must be designated in each state where you will operate. A process agent receives legal documents on behalf of your company. You can use a third-party service for all states where you do not operate a business base or designate an individual within your company as long as your business base is in the same state.

    For example, if your business is in Ohio, you or your company designee, can be the business's processing agent, however if you do not have a business base, in other states outside of Ohio, a processing agent must be obtained typically through a third-party.

5. Pay Application Fee
    There is an application fee for MC authority, which varies based on the type of authority and your operations. Payment options will be provided during the application process. Typically, there is a $300/PER MC AUTHORITY APPLIED FOR.

    For example, if your business would like to obtain an operating authority for Motor Carrier of Property AND Motor Passenger Carrier Authority, expect to pay $600 for the application fee.

6. Submit Proof of Insurance
    Submit proof of liability insurance (Form BMC-91 or BMC-91X) to the FMCSA. The insurance must meet minimum requirements set by the FMCSA. This must be completed by your insurance company, so when shopping for insurance, it's important to ensure the insurance agent/company has the capabilities to get this completed. Not completing this necessary step can result in your application being declined, with NO REFUND of the application fee.

7. Wait Patiently
    After submitting your application, the FMCSA will review it for completeness and compliance with regulations. This process can take several weeks.

8. Receive MC Authority
    Once your application is approved, you will receive your MC authority, which includes an MC number (and FF number if applicable). This allows you to legally operate as a motor carrier.

By following these steps and ensuring all requirements are met, you can obtain MC authority from the FMCSA and legally operate as a motor carrier in the United States.

OBTAINING YOUR MC AUTHORITY WEEKLY SCHEDULE

WEEK OF:

STEP 1

CREATE A FMCSA PORTAL ACCOUNT

VISIT THE FMCSA'S UNIFIED REGISTRATION SYSTEM (URS) ONLINE PORTAL AND CREATE AN ACCOUNT

STEP 2

AFTER LOGGING IN, COMPLETE THE APPLICATION FOR MC AUTHORITY:

SELECT THE APPROPRIATE AUTHORITY TYPE (MC OR FF)

STEP 3

DESIGNATE PROCESS AGENTS

STEP 4

PAY APPLICATION FEE

STEP 5

SUBMIT PROOF OF INSURANCE

STEP 6

WAIT PATIENTLY TO RECEIVE MC AUTHORITY

NOTE:

Commercial Transportation Insurance Strategies

Finding commercial trucking insurance can be a complex task due to the specialized nature of the industry and the specific insurance needs involved. Here are some helpful strategies to guide you through the process:

❖ Understand Your Insurance Needs
- ➢ Type of Coverage: Determine the specific types of coverage you need, such as liability insurance, physical damage coverage, cargo insurance, and uninsured/underinsured motorist coverage.
- ➢ Federal and State Requirements: Familiarize yourself with the minimum insurance requirements mandated by the Federal Motor Carrier Safety Administration (FMCSA) and state authorities where you operate.

❖ Work with Specialized Insurance Providers
- ➢ Trucking Insurance Specialists: Look for insurance companies or brokers that specialize in commercial trucking insurance. They understand the unique risks and requirements of the industry and can provide tailored coverage options.
- ➢ Membership Associations: Consider joining industry associations like the Owner-Operator Independent Drivers Association (OOIDA), which may offer access to group insurance programs tailored for trucking professionals.

❖ Compare Multiple Quotes
- ➢ Shop Around: Obtain quotes from multiple insurance providers to compare coverage options, premiums, deductibles, and policy terms.
- ➢ Online Tools and Brokers: Utilize online insurance comparison tools or work with insurance brokers who can gather quotes from multiple carriers on your behalf.

❖ Evaluate Insurance Providers
- ➢ Financial Stability: Verify the financial stability and reputation of insurance companies by checking ratings from agencies like A.M. Best, Moody's, or Standard & Poor's.
- ➢ Customer Reviews: Read reviews and testimonials from other trucking professionals to gauge customer satisfaction and claims handling experience.

❖ Review Policy Coverage and Exclusions
- ➢ Policy Details: Carefully review the coverage limits, exclusions, endorsements, and any additional benefits offered by each insurance policy.
- ➢ Customizable Options: Look for insurers that offer customizable coverage options to tailor policies to your specific needs, such as seasonal adjustments or specialized cargo coverage.
- ➢ Remember, typical coverage includes general liability, auto liability, and cargo liability coverage

❖ Consider Safety and Risk Management Programs
- ➢ Safety Programs: Implementing safety measures and training programs within your business can help reduce insurance premiums. Many insurers offer discounts for fleets with strong safety records.
- ➢ Risk Management: Discuss risk management strategies with insurance providers to minimize risks and potential claims, which can positively impact your insurance premiums.

❖ Seek Professional Advice
- ➢ Insurance Agents/Brokers: Work with experienced insurance agents or brokers who specialize in commercial trucking. They can provide expert guidance, help navigate complex insurance terms, and negotiate favorable terms on your behalf.

- ❖ Review and Renew Regularly
  - ➢ Annual Review: Regularly review your insurance coverage to ensure it meets your evolving business needs and remains competitive in terms of pricing and coverage.
  - ➢ Renewal Negotiations: Don't hesitate to negotiate renewal terms with your insurer based on your updated claims history and business performance.

By following these strategies, you can effectively navigate the process of finding commercial trucking insurance, ensuring that your business is adequately protected against risks while maintaining compliance with regulatory requirements.

Registering for International Fuel Tax Agreement

IFTA (International Fuel Tax Agreement) is an agreement between U.S. states and Canadian provinces that simplifies the reporting and payment of motor fuel taxes for interstate and inter-jurisdictional motor carriers. Under IFTA, the responsibility for paying fuel taxes lies with the motor carrier. IFTA was established in 1983 to simplify and standardize the reporting and payment of fuel taxes by motor carriers operating in multiple jurisdictions. It was adopted to replace the cumbersome process of obtaining fuel permits from each state or province separately. As of 2024, there are 48 contiguous U.S. states and 10 Canadian provinces that participate in IFTA. The agreement does not include Alaska, Hawaii, or the Canadian territories. Fuel taxes collected under IFTA are distributed among participating jurisdictions based on the mileage traveled by carriers in each jurisdiction. This ensures that states and provinces receive their fair share of fuel tax revenue from interstate commerce. IFTA plays a crucial role in facilitating interstate commerce by providing a standardized method for fuel tax reporting and payment. This helps maintain fairness and consistency in taxation for motor carriers operating across state and provincial borders.

Reminders:

- It is the Motor Carrier's responsibility: The motor carrier that operates qualified motor vehicles across state or provincial lines is responsible for registering under IFTA, filing quarterly tax returns, and paying the applicable fuel taxes to their base jurisdiction (the jurisdiction where the carrier is registered).
- Base Jurisdiction Selection: Each motor carrier must designate a base jurisdiction where they register for IFTA. This jurisdiction issues the IFTA license and provides the necessary reporting forms. The carrier reports all taxable fuel purchases and mileage accrued in all jurisdictions (states or provinces) during the reporting period to their base jurisdiction.
- Quarterly Reporting and Payment: Motor carriers must file quarterly IFTA tax returns with their base jurisdiction, reporting the total distance traveled and total fuel consumed in each jurisdiction. They calculate and remit any fuel taxes owed or receive a refund if they have overpaid.
- Audits and Compliance: IFTA jurisdictions conduct audits to ensure compliance with reporting and payment requirements. Audits verify that carriers accurately reported fuel purchases and mileage and paid the correct amount of fuel taxes based on their operations.
- Penalties for Non-compliance: Failure to comply with IFTA reporting and payment requirements can result in penalties, fines, and potential suspension of the carrier's IFTA license. It's essential for carriers to maintain accurate records and adhere to filing deadlines.

Remember, the motor carrier is directly responsible for registering under IFTA, maintaining records of fuel purchases and mileage, filing quarterly tax returns, and remitting fuel taxes to their base jurisdiction based on their interstate and inter-jurisdictional operations. This responsibility ensures uniformity and efficiency in fuel tax collection across multiple jurisdictions.

Registering for International Fuel Tax Agreement

Listed below are the steps to obtain credentials that allow interstate motor carriers to report and pay taxes on motor fuel used in member jurisdictions. Remember if you're an intrastate motor carrier, this step is not required.

1. Ensure your business meets the criteria to qualify for IFTA:
    - Operates qualified motor vehicles (typically vehicles with two axles and a GVWR exceeding 26,000 pounds or vehicles with three or more axles regardless of weight).
    - Engages in interstate commerce (crosses state lines) or operates within Canada or Mexico.
- Contact the motor vehicle agency in your base jurisdiction to apply for an IFTA license:
    - Obtain the IFTA license application form from your state's motor vehicle agency website or office.
    - Complete the application form with accurate information about your business and vehicles.
- Provide Required Documentation
    - Proof of vehicle ownership or lease agreements.
    - Federal Employer Identification Number (EIN) or Social Security Number (SSN).
    - USDOT number (if applicable).
    - Proof of insurance.
- Submit the completed application and required documentation
- Pay the applicable fees for the IFTA license and decals:
    - Fees vary by jurisdiction and may include an initial application fee and an annual renewal fee.
    - Some states also require a bond or deposit.
- Once your application is approved and fees are paid, you will receive:
    - IFTA license: This allows you to operate under the IFTA agreement.
    - IFTA decals: These are typically stickers that you affix to your vehicles to indicate compliance with IFTA.

Additional Tips:
- Stay Compliant: Ensure you comply with IFTA reporting requirements to avoid penalties or fines.
- Renew: Renew your IFTA license annually and update any changes to your business or vehicle information promptly.
- Keep Records: Maintain accurate records of fuel purchases and miles traveled in each jurisdiction for auditing purposes.

By following these steps and fulfilling all requirements, you can register for IFTA plates and operate your vehicles under the International Fuel Tax Agreement efficiently and legally. For specific details and forms, consult your base jurisdiction's motor vehicle agency or their website.

INTERNATIONAL FUEL TAX AGREEMENT REMINDERS

ENSURE YOUR BUSINESS MEETS THE CRITERIA TO QUALIFY FOR IFTA

CONTACT THE MOTOR VEHICLE AGENCY IN YOUR BASE JURISDICTION TO APPLY FOR AN IFTA LICENSE

PROVIDE REQUIRED DOCUMENTATION

SUBMIT THE COMPLETED APPLICATION AND REQUIRED DOCUMENTATION

PAY THE APPLICABLE FEES FOR THE IFTA LICENSE AND DECALS

ONCE YOUR APPLICATION IS APPROVED AND FEES ARE PAID, YOU WILL RECEIVE LICENSE AND DECALS

AFTER RECEIVING YOUR IFTA LICENSE AND DECALS, YOU MUST FILE QUARTERLY FUEL TAX RETURNS WITH YOUR BASE JURISDICTION'S MOTOR VEHICLE AGENCY AND REPORT THE AMOUNT OF FUEL PURCHASED AND CONSUMED IN EACH JURISDICTION TRAVELED.

Registering for International Registration Plan

The International Registration Plan (IRP) is an agreement among the U.S. and Canadian provinces with the purpose to simplify the registration process for commercial vehicles that operate in multiple jurisdictions, establish uniform registration requirements and fee structures across jurisdictions, and ensure fees paid are distributed among the jurisdictions based on the proportion of miles traveled in each jurisdiction by the carrier's fleet. The IRP promotes uniformity, fairness in fee distribution, facilitates interstate commerce, and supports regulatory compliance for motor carriers.

How to guide of registering for the IRP:

1. Ensure the commercial vehicle(s) meet the eligibility criteria for IRP registration. Typically, vehicles qualify if they:
   - ☐ Have a gross vehicle weight (GVW) or registered gross vehicle weight (RGVW) exceeding 26,000 pounds (11,793.4 kg) or have three or more axles (regardless of weight).
   - ☐ Intended for transporting goods or passengers across state or provincial lines.

2. Select a base jurisdiction where your business is located, where your vehicles are based, or where operational control of your fleet is maintained. This jurisdiction will handle your IRP registration and fee collection.

3. Collect information about your business and vehicles, including:
   - ☐ Vehicle identification numbers (VINs)
   - ☐ Gross vehicle weight (GVW) or registered gross vehicle weight (RGVW)
   - ☐ Proof of vehicle ownership or lease agreement
   - ☐ Business contact information and tax identification number (EIN)

4. Complete the Application
   - ☐ Obtain the IRP application form from your chosen base jurisdiction's motor vehicle agency or download it from their website.
   - ☐ Complete the application accurately and provide all required information about your business and each vehicle you intend to register under IRP.

5. Calculate the registration fees based on the total distance your vehicles are expected to travel in each jurisdiction covered by IRP. Fees are typically determined by a formula that considers vehicle weight and the proportion of miles traveled in each jurisdiction.

6. Submit the Application
   - ☐ Submit your completed IRP application form and any required supporting documents to your base jurisdiction's motor vehicle agency.
   - ☐ Pay the applicable registration fees along with your application submission. Fees can usually be paid by check, money order, or electronic payment methods accepted by the jurisdiction.

7. Once your application is processed and fees are paid, you will receive:
   - ☐ IRP cab card: This card must be carried in each registered vehicle at all times as proof of valid registration.

	☐ IRP registration plates: Some jurisdictions issue special plates that indicate the vehicle's participation in IRP.
8.	Renew your IRP registration annually. This typically involves submitting renewal applications and paying renewal fees to your base jurisdiction.
9.	Keep accurate records of mileage traveled in each jurisdiction to facilitate accurate reporting during annual renewals and audits.

Registering for IRP
International Fuel Tax

1. Ensure the commercial vehicle(s) meet the eligibility criteria for IRP registration
2. Select a base jurisdiction where your business is located
3. Collect information about your business and vehicles
4. Complete the Application
5. Calculate the registration fees
6. Submit the Application
7. Receive cab card & plates
8. Renew your IRP registration annually
9. Keep accurate records of mileage

 **Dont forget to use your Transportation Guidebook for specifics**

Vehicles & Equipment in the Trucking Industry

The trucking industry relies on various types of vehicles to transport goods across different distances and terrains. Some common types of vehicles used in the trucking industry include:

- Semi-trailer trucks (Semi-trucks or Tractor-trailers): These are the most common type of trucks seen on highways. They consist of a tractor unit (often called a cab or tractor) that pulls one or more trailers. The trailers can vary in size and type, including dry vans, flatbeds, refrigerated trailers (reefers), tankers for liquids, and specialized trailers for specific cargo.

- Straight trucks: These are trucks with a single rigid frame and no separate trailer. They often have a cabin for the driver and a cargo area, making them suitable for local or regional deliveries.

- Dump trucks: These trucks are designed to transport loose materials, such as sand, gravel, or demolition debris. They have an open-box bed that is lifted at the front end to dump the contents.

- Tank trucks: Also known as tankers, these trucks are designed to transport liquids or gases. They have cylindrical tanks mounted on the truck chassis, often with special features to handle hazardous materials or temperature-sensitive liquids.

- Flatbed trucks: These trucks have a flat, open bed without sides or a roof, making them suitable for transporting large or oversized items that do not fit inside a standard enclosed trailer.

- Refrigerated trucks (Reefers): These trucks have insulated bodies and refrigeration units to transport perishable goods at controlled temperatures. They are essential for transporting items like fresh produce, dairy products, and pharmaceuticals.

- Parcel delivery vans: These are smaller vehicles used by courier and delivery companies to transport packages and parcels to residential and commercial locations.

> Specialized vehicles: Depending on the specific requirements of the cargo being transported, the trucking industry also uses specialized vehicles such as car carriers (for transporting cars), livestock trailers (for transporting animals), and heavy haul trucks (for transporting oversized or overweight loads).

In addition to the common types of trucks used in the industry, there are several specialized vehicles and equipment designed for specific purposes within the trucking and transportation sector. These specialized vehicles cater to unique cargo needs, operational requirements, and safety regulations. Here are some examples:

> Car Carriers: These are specialized trailers designed to transport automobiles. They can range from small trailers that carry a few cars to large multi-level trailers capable of transporting dozens of vehicles.

> Livestock Trailers: These trailers are specifically designed to transport livestock, such as cattle, horses, and pigs. They provide ventilation, partitions, and flooring designed for the comfort and safety of the animals during transportation.

> Tanker Trucks: Tankers are used to transport liquids or gases, including fuels (like gasoline and diesel), chemicals, milk, and industrial gases. They come in various sizes and configurations depending on the type of cargo and regulatory requirements.

> Refrigerated Trailers (Reefers): Reefers are equipped with refrigeration units and insulated walls to transport perishable goods such as fresh produce, dairy products, pharmaceuticals, and frozen foods. They maintain specific temperature ranges to preserve the quality and safety of the cargo.

> Flatbed Trailers: Flatbeds have an open, flat platform without sides or a roof, making them suitable for transporting oversized or irregularly shaped cargo. They are commonly used for transporting construction materials, machinery, and large equipment.

> Dry Van Trailers: These trailers are enclosed and used for transporting general cargo that needs protection from the elements. They are versatile and commonly used for transporting consumer goods, electronics, and packaged goods.

- ➢ Double and Triple Trailers: These configurations involve coupling multiple trailers to a single tractor unit. Double trailers consist of two trailers, while triple trailers have three trailers. They are used for maximizing cargo capacity and efficiency on long-haul routes, primarily in regions with specific regulatory allowances.

- ➢ Intermodal Containers: These standardized containers are used for intermodal transportation, allowing goods to be easily transferred between different modes of transport (such as truck, rail, and ship) without needing to unload and reload the cargo.
- ➢ Heavy Haul Trucks: These are specialized trucks designed to transport oversized or overweight loads that exceed standard legal limits. They may require special permits and escorts due to their size and weight.

- ➢ Tow Trucks: These trucks are equipped with mechanisms for towing and recovering vehicles that are disabled, abandoned, or illegally parked. They are essential for roadside assistance and vehicle recovery services.

These specialized vehicles and equipment play crucial roles in meeting the diverse transportation needs of industries ranging from agriculture and construction to retail and logistics. Each type is designed with specific features and capabilities to ensure the safe and efficient transport of various types of cargo under different conditions and regulatory requirements. Different commodities require different types of equipment in the trucking industry primarily due to their unique characteristics, handling requirements, and regulatory considerations. Here's how various commodities dictate the choice of equipment:

- ➢ Perishable Goods (Refrigerated Products):
    - ❖ Equipment Needed: Refrigerated trailers (reefers) equipped with cooling systems.
    - ❖ Reason: Perishable goods such as fresh produce, dairy products, and pharmaceuticals require temperature-controlled environments to maintain freshness and prevent spoilage during transportation.

- ➢ Bulk Liquids (Chemicals, Fuels):
    - ❖ Equipment Needed: Tanker trucks with specialized tanks.
    - ❖ Reason: Tanker trucks are designed to transport liquids safely, with tanks that can withstand the specific requirements of hazardous materials or the temperature control needed for sensitive liquids like chemicals and food-grade products.

- Automobiles:
  - ❖ Equipment Needed: Car carriers or flatbed trailers.
  - ❖ Reason: Car carriers are designed with ramps and securements to transport vehicles safely without damage. Flatbed trailers may also be used for transporting vehicles that need to be driven on and off.

- Construction Materials (Lumber, Steel):
  - ❖ Equipment Needed: Flatbed trailers, sometimes with side kits or tarps.
  - ❖ Reason: Flatbed trailers allow for easy loading and unloading of large, heavy, or irregularly shaped items such as lumber, steel beams, and construction equipment. Side kits or tarps provide protection from the weather.

- Livestock:
  - ❖ Equipment Needed: Livestock trailers with appropriate ventilation and partitions.
  - ❖ Reason: Livestock trailers are designed to ensure the comfort and safety of animals during transportation, with features that minimize stress and prevent injuries.

- Dry Goods (Consumer Products, Packaged Goods):
  - ❖ Equipment Needed: Dry van trailers.
  - ❖ Reason: Dry van trailers provide enclosed and secure transport for general cargo, protecting goods from weather conditions and theft while providing ease of loading and unloading at distribution centers and retail locations.

- Oversized or Overweight Cargo:
  - ❖ Equipment Needed: Heavy haul trucks or specialized trailers with permits.
  - ❖ Reason: Cargo that exceeds standard legal limits requires specialized equipment and permits to ensure safe transport, compliance with regulations, and minimal disruption to traffic and infrastructure.

- Intermodal Transportation:
  - ❖ Equipment Needed: Intermodal containers compatible with trucks, trains, and ships.
  - ❖ Reason: Intermodal containers provide standardized transport units that can be easily transferred between different modes of transportation without the need to unload and reload cargo, reducing handling costs and transit times.

➤ Fragile Goods (Electronics, Artwork):
❖ Equipment Needed: Climate-controlled trailers or specialized packaging.
❖ Reason: Fragile goods require careful handling and protection from shocks, vibrations, and temperature fluctuations. Climate-controlled trailers or specialized packaging ensure that these items arrive intact and in optimal condition.

Each type of equipment is tailored to meet specific requirements related to the nature of the cargo, ensuring efficient and safe transportation while complying with regulatory standards and industry best practices. Adapting the right equipment for each commodity helps minimize risks, preserve product quality, and optimize logistical operations in the trucking industry.

Vehicles & Equipment in the Trucking Industry

Securing cargo properly is crucial to ensure it arrives safely at its destination. Here are some recommended types of supplies used to secure cargo:

- Straps and Tie-Downs:
    - Purpose: Used to secure cargo to prevent shifting and movement.
    - Types: Ratchet straps, cam buckle straps, winch straps, and webbing straps made from materials like polyester or nylon.

- Chains and Binders:
    - Purpose: Provide heavy-duty securing for larger or heavier cargo.
    - Types: Grade 70 transport chains, binders (lever or ratchet), and chain hooks.

- Load Bars and Cargo Bars:
    - Purpose: Used to brace cargo against walls or other cargo to prevent shifting.
    - Types: Adjustable load bars, cargo bars with spring mechanisms, and E-track load bars for use in trailers.

- Cargo Nets:
    - Purpose: Secure irregularly shaped cargo or loose items.
    - Types: Webbing cargo nets with hooks, bungee-style nets, and custom-sized nets for specific cargo dimensions.

- Dunnage Bags:
    - Purpose: Fill voids and stabilize cargo to prevent movement.
    - Types: Inflatable dunnage bags made from materials like polyethylene or woven polypropylene, available in various sizes and pressure ratings.

- Edge and Corner Protectors:
    - Purpose: Protect cargo from straps and tie-downs, preventing damage during transit.
    - Types: Plastic edge protectors, cardboard corner protectors, and foam edge guards.

- ➢ Pallets and Skids:
  - ❖ Purpose: Provide a stable base for stacking and securing cargo.
  - ❖ Types: Wooden pallets, plastic pallets, and metal skids of various sizes and configurations.

Vehicles & Equipment in the Trucking Industry

- ➢ Strapping Tools and Accessories:
  - ❖ Purpose: Aid in tensioning, cutting, and securing straps and tie-downs.
  - ❖ Types: Tensioning tools (manual or pneumatic), cutters, corner protectors for straps, and edge guards for webbing.

- ➢ Shrink Wrap and Stretch Wrap:
  - ❖ Purpose: Protect cargo from moisture, dust, and tampering.
  - ❖ Types: Stretch wrap rolls (hand or machine-applied) and shrink wrap films for heat-shrinking.

- ➢ Anti-Slip Mats and Liners:
  - ❖ Purpose: Provide traction and prevent sliding of cargo.
  - ❖ Types: Rubber anti-slip mats, adhesive-backed liners, and non-slip pallet liners.

- ➢ Locks and Seals:
  - ❖ Purpose: Secure containers and trailers to prevent unauthorized access and tampering.
  - ❖ Types: Padlocks, high-security seals, bolt seals, and cable seals for containers and trailer doors.

- ➢ Braces and Blocks:
  - ❖ Purpose: Provide additional support and prevent movement of heavy or delicate cargo.
  - ❖ Types: Wooden or plastic braces, chocks, and blocks tailored to fit cargo dimensions.

These supplies are essential for ensuring that cargo is securely packed and transported, minimizing the risk of damage, loss, or accidents during transit. Proper use of these supplies also helps logistics providers comply with safety regulations and meet customer expectations for cargo integrity and delivery reliability.

Trucking Company Website Passwords

Website	Login	Password

We hope this step-by-step guidebook was helpful in assisting you with understanding how to register your business with any Secretary of State, and why specific federal and state steps are required with getting started in the transportation industry.

Our goal is always to assist entrepreneurs with being successful, not being fearful to jump into a new viable market, and we enjoy providing business owners with tools where, even if they don't start off that way, they can end up independently managing their company.

Some key takeaways to remember is:

- *Owning a business allows you to be your own boss, making decisions that align with your values and vision without being subject to the demands or limitations of an employer.*
- *Starting a business enables you to work in a field you're passionate about. Turning a hobby or interest into a business can make your work more fulfilling and enjoyable.*
- *Running a business involves learning new skills and gaining knowledge in areas such as marketing, finance, and operations. This ongoing learning process can be intellectually stimulating and rewarding.*
- *Business owners can take advantage of various tax deductions and incentives not available to employees. These can include deductions for home office expenses, travel, equipment, and health insurance.*

Starting your own business is a powerful way to take control of your career, pursue your passions, and potentially achieve financial success. While it requires hard work, dedication, and a willingness to take risks, the rewards—both personal and financial—can be substantial. Whether you're driven by the desire for independence, the chance to innovate, or the goal of creating a legacy, entrepreneurship offers a unique path to fulfillment and success.

The steps in our guide may seem daunting, but remember, owning and operating a transportation company can actually be highly profitable! Our goal is for your transportation business to have paramount success and longevity.

Remember, you've got this!

For more information or guidance, please contact:

MSW Enterprise Ltd. Logistic & Transportation Professional Services

Our website:

https://mswenterpriseltd.com/

www.ingramcontent.com/pod-product-compliance
Lightning Source LLC
Chambersburg PA
CBHW040334220526
45473CB00009B/2676